seafood	
chicken	
meat	
pasta	46
rice	54
glossary	60
conversion chart	62
index	63

contents

Please note that Australian cup and spoon measurements are metric.
A conversion chart appears on page 62.

seafood

fish with chunky tomato, anchovy and caper sauce

1 tablespoon olive oil
4 x 200g firm white fish fillets
1 medium brown onion (150g), chopped finely
2 cloves garlic, crushed
4 medium tomatoes (600g), peeled, seeded, chopped coarsely
4 drained anchovy fillets, chopped finely
1 tablespoon rinsed, drained capers
1 teaspoon white sugar
¼ cup coarsely chopped fresh flat-leaf parsley

1 Heat half the oil in large frying pan; cook fish, uncovered, until cooked as desired.
2 Meanwhile, heat remaining oil in small saucepan; cook onion and garlic, stirring, until onion softens. Add tomato; cook, stirring, 1 minute. Remove from heat; stir in anchovy, capers, sugar and parsley. Top fish with sauce; serve with a leafy green salad and lemon wedges, if you like.

preparation time 15 minutes
cooking time 15 minutes
serves 4
nutritional count per serving 7.1g total fat (1.1g saturated fat); 1099kJ (263 cal); 6.4g carbohydrate; 41.8g protein; 2.8g fibre

note We used blue-eye fillets in this recipe, but you can use any firm white fish fillets you like. Bream, whiting, flathead, swordfish, ling, jewfish, snapper or sea perch are all good choices.

seafood

spiced fried fish

1 tablespoon plain flour
1½ teaspoons ground cumin
1½ teaspoons ground coriander
1 teaspoon sweet smoked paprika
¼ teaspoon cayenne pepper
8 bream fillets (800g)
1 tablespoon olive oil

lemon pistachio couscous
1 cup (200g) couscous
¾ cup (180ml) boiling water
2 teaspoons finely grated lemon rind
¼ cup (60ml) lemon juice
½ cup (70g) pistachios
2 teaspoons olive oil
1 garlic clove, crushed
1 small red onion (100g), finely chopped
½ cup coarsely chopped fresh mint

1 Combine flour and spices in medium bowl; add fish, rub mixture all over fish.
2 Heat oil in large frying pan; cook fish, in batches, until browned and cooked as desired.
3 Make lemon pistachio couscous.
4 Serve fish with couscous.
lemon pistachio couscous Combine couscous, water, rind and juice in medium heatproof bowl. Cover; stand 5 minutes or until liquid is absorbed, fluffing with fork occasionally. Meanwhile, heat small frying pan; dry-fry nuts until fragrant. Remove nuts from pan. Heat oil in same pan, add garlic and onion; cook, stirring, until onion softens. Stir nuts, onion mixture and mint through couscous.

preparation time 10 minutes
cooking time 15 minutes
serves 4
nutritional count per serving
25.4g total fat (5.5g saturated fat); 2571kJ (614 cal); 43g carbohydrate; 49.7g protein; 2.9g fibre
note We used bream fillets here, but you can use any firm white fish fillet, such as perch, blue-eye or ling, if you prefer.

seafood

fish cutlets with mango salsa

4 x 200g firm white fish cutlets
2 tablespoons lime juice
1 tablespoon fish sauce
1 tablespoon peanut oil
1 tablespoon grated palm sugar
1 teaspoon sambal oelek
2 kaffir lime leaves, shredded finely
mango salsa
2 large mangoes (1.2kg), chopped coarsely
2 lebanese cucumbers (260g), seeded, chopped coarsely
1 fresh long red chilli, seeded, sliced thinly
½ cup coarsely chopped fresh mint

1 Make mango salsa.
2 Cook fish, in batches, on heated oiled grill plate (or grill or barbecue) until browned both sides and cooked as desired.
3 Place remaining ingredients in screw-top jar; shake well. Divide salsa and fish among serving plates; drizzle with dressing.
mango salsa Place ingredients in medium bowl; toss gently to combine.

preparation time 15 minutes
cooking time 15 minutes
serves 4
nutritional count per serving 8.7g total fat (2g saturated fat); 1501kJ (359 cal); 31.8g carbohydrate; 35.7g protein; 4.3g fibre
note We used blue-eye cutlets in this recipe, but you can use any white fish cutlets you like. Bream, flathead, swordfish, ling, snapper or sea perch are all good choices.

seafood

grilled snapper fillets with fennel and onion salad

1 medium red onion (170g), sliced thinly
4 green onions, sliced thinly
1 large fennel bulb (550g), trimmed, sliced thinly
2 stalks celery (300g), trimmed, sliced thinly
½ cup coarsely chopped fresh flat-leaf parsley
⅓ cup (80ml) orange juice
¼ cup (60ml) olive oil
2 cloves garlic, crushed
2 teaspoons sambal oelek
4 x 275g snapper fillets, skin on

1 Combine onions, fennel, celery and parsley in medium bowl.
2 Place juice, oil, garlic and sambal in screw-top jar; shake well.
3 Cook fish on heated oiled grill plate (or grill or barbecue) until browned both sides and cooked as desired.
4 Pour half the dressing over salad in bowl; toss gently to combine. Serve salad topped with fish; drizzle with remaining dressing.

preparation time 15 minutes
cooking time 10 minutes
serves 4
nutritional count per serving 18.3g total fat (3.3g saturated fat); 1580kJ (378 cal); 8g carbohydrate; 43g protein; 4.5g fibre

chicken

pesto chicken with grilled zucchini

6 medium zucchini (720g), sliced thinly lengthways
2 tablespoons olive oil
1 clove garlic, crushed
1 tablespoon finely chopped fresh basil
1 teaspoon finely grated lemon rind
⅓ cup (90g) sun-dried tomato pesto
2 tablespoons chicken stock
4 x 200g chicken thigh fillets, cut into thirds

1 Cook zucchini on heated oiled grill plate (or grill or barbecue), in batches, until tender. Combine with oil, garlic, basil and rind in medium bowl; cover to keep warm.
2 Combine pesto, stock and chicken in large bowl. Cook chicken on heated oiled grill plate (or grill or barbecue), brushing occasionally with pesto mixture, until cooked. Serve chicken with zucchini, and rocket leaves, if you like.

preparation time 10 minutes
cooking time 15 minutes
serves 4
nutritional count per serving 33.1g total fat (7.6g saturated fat); 2611kJ (481 cal); 3.3g carbohydrate; 41.7g protein; 3.6g fibre

note We used a 400g packet of asian stir-fry vegetables for this recipe, available from most supermarkets.

chicken

ginger-plum chicken and noodle stir-fry

2 tablespoons vegetable oil
600g chicken breast fillets, sliced thinly
450g hokkien noodles
1 medium brown onion (150g), sliced thinly
1 clove garlic, crushed
3cm piece fresh ginger (15g), grated
400g packaged fresh asian stir-fry vegetables
2 tablespoons sweet chilli sauce
2 tablespoons plum sauce

1 Heat half the oil in wok; stir-fry chicken, in batches, until browned.
2 Meanwhile, place noodles in medium heatproof bowl, cover with boiling water; separate with fork, drain.
3 Heat remaining oil in wok; stir-fry onion, garlic and ginger until onion softens. Add vegetables; stir-fry until just tender. Return chicken to wok with noodles and sauces; stir-fry until hot.

preparation time 10 minutes
cooking time 15 minutes
serves 4
nutritional count per serving 19.4g total fat (4.6g saturated fat); 2784kJ (666 cal); 73.3g carbohydrate; 45.6g protein; 6.2g fibre

chicken

chicken margherita

550g baby vine-ripened truss tomatoes
4 x 200g chicken breast fillets
⅓ cup (90g) basil pesto
180g bocconcini cheese, sliced thinly
20g baby spinach leaves
8 slices prosciutto (120g)

1 Preheat oven to 220°C/200°C fan-forced.
2 Remove four tomatoes from truss; slice thinly.
3 Split one chicken fillet in half horizontally; open out. Spread one tablespoon of pesto on one side of chicken fillet; top with a quarter of the cheese, a quarter of the sliced tomato and a quarter of the spinach. Fold chicken fillet over filling; wrap with two slices prosciutto to enclose securely. Repeat process with remaining chicken, pesto, cheese, sliced tomato, spinach and prosciutto.
4 Roast chicken and remaining tomatoes in oiled large shallow baking dish, uncovered, about 20 minutes or until cooked through. Serve chicken with roasted tomatoes.

preparation time 10 minutes
cooking time 20 minutes
serves 4
nutritional count per serving 28.7g total fat (10.5g saturated fat); 2144kJ (513 cal); 3g carbohydrate; 59.7g protein; 2.3g fibre

tip Parmigiana goes well with homemade chips. Cut 1kg unpeeled potatoes into 2cm-thick chips; boil, steam or microwave until just tender. Drain, then dry with absorbent paper. Toss in large bowl with 1 tablespoon olive oil; place, in a single layer, on oiled oven tray. Roast in preheated 240°C/220°C fan-forced oven about 25 minutes or until browned.

chicken

spinach and ricotta-stuffed chicken parmigiana

4 chicken breast fillets (800g)
40g baby spinach leaves
1⅓ cups (320g) ricotta cheese
¼ cup (35g) plain flour
2 eggs
2 tablespoons milk
1½ cups (105g) stale breadcrumbs
vegetable oil, for shallow-frying
1 cup (260g) bottled tomato pasta sauce
1 cup (100g) coarsely grated mozzarella cheese

1 Preheat oven to 200°C/180°C fan-forced. Oil shallow large baking dish.
2 Using meat mallet, gently pound chicken, one piece at a time, between sheets of plastic wrap until 5mm thick; cut each piece in half.
3 Top each schnitzel with spinach and cheese, leaving 1cm border around edges. Fold in half to cover filling; press down firmly then secure with toothpicks.
4 Coat schnitzels in flour; shake off excess. Dip in combined egg and milk, then in breadcrumbs.
5 Heat oil in large frying pan; cook schnitzels, in batches, until browned and cooked through. Drain on absorbent paper.
6 Place schnitzels in baking dish; top with sauce and cheese. Roast, uncovered, in oven, 10 minutes or until cheese melts.

preparation time 15 minutes
cooking time 20 minutes
serves 4
nutritional count per serving
40.2g total fat (15.3g saturated fat); 3194kJ (764 cal); 31.9g carbohydrate; 67.2g protein; 2.9g fibre

chicken

herbed chicken schnitzel

4 chicken breast fillets (800g)
¼ cup (35g) plain flour
2 eggs
1 tablespoon milk
2½ cups (175g) stale white breadcrumbs
2 teaspoons finely grated lemon rind
2 tablespoons finely chopped fresh flat-leaf parsley
2 tablespoons finely chopped fresh basil
⅓ cup (25g) finely grated parmesan cheese
vegetable oil, for shallow-frying
green bean salad
250g baby green beans, trimmed
2 tablespoons lemon juice
1 tablespoon olive oil
⅓ cup coarsely chopped fresh flat-leaf parsley

1 Using meat mallet, gently pound chicken, one piece at a time, between sheets of plastic wrap until 5mm thick; cut each piece in half.
2 Whisk flour, eggs and milk in shallow bowl; combine breadcrumbs, rind, herbs and cheese in another shallow bowl. Coat chicken pieces, one at a time, in egg mixture then in breadcrumb mixture.
3 Heat oil in large frying pan; shallow-fry chicken, in batches, until cooked. Drain on absorbent paper.
4 Meanwhile, make green bean salad; serve salad with chicken, and lemon wedges, if you like.
green bean salad Boil, steam or microwave beans until tender; drain. Toss beans in medium bowl with remaining ingredients.

preparation time 20 minutes
cooking time 15 minutes
serves 4
nutritional count per serving 28.1g total fat (5.9g saturated fat); 2746kJ (657 cal); 38.5g carbohydrate; 59.9g protein; 4.6g fibre

meat

spicy beef and bean salad

¼ cup (60ml) olive oil
35g packet taco seasoning mix
600g piece beef eye fillet
2 tablespoons lime juice
1 clove garlic, crushed
420g can four-bean mix, rinsed, drained
310g can corn kernels, rinsed, drained
2 lebanese cucumbers (260g), chopped finely
1 small red onion (100g), chopped finely
1 large red capsicum (350g), chopped finely
½ cup coarsely chopped fresh coriander
1 fresh long red chilli, chopped finely

1 Combine 1 tablespoon of the oil, the seasoning and beef in medium bowl. Cook beef on heated oiled grill plate (or grill or barbecue) until cooked as desired. Cover, stand 5 minutes then slice thinly.
2 Meanwhile, whisk remaining oil, juice and garlic in large bowl. Add remaining ingredients; toss gently to combine. Serve beef with salad; sprinkle with fresh coriander leaves, if desired.

preparation time 10 minutes
cooking time 20 minutes
serves 4
nutritional count per serving 22.2g total fat (5.2g saturated fat); 2111kJ (505 cal); 30.9g carbohydrate; 40.4g protein; 9.3g fibre

meat

fajitas with guacamole and salsa cruda

3 cloves garlic, crushed
¼ cup (60ml) lemon juice
2 teaspoons ground cumin
1 tablespoon olive oil
600g piece beef eye fillet, sliced thinly
1 large red capsicum (350g), sliced thinly
1 large green capsicum (350g), sliced thinly
1 medium yellow capsicum (200g), sliced thinly
1 large red onion (300g), sliced thinly
8 large flour tortillas (460g)
guacamole
1 large avocado (320g)
1 tablespoon lime juice
1 small white onion (80g)
¼ cup fresh coriander
salsa cruda
2 medium tomatoes (300g)
1 fresh long red chilli
1 small white onion (80g)
1 tablespoon lime juice
½ cup coarsely chopped fresh coriander

1 Combine garlic, juice, cumin, oil and beef in large bowl, cover; refrigerate.
2 Make guacamole. Make salsa cruda.
3 Cook beef, in batches, in heated oiled large frying pan until cooked as desired. Remove from pan; cover to keep warm.
4 Cook capsicums and onion in same pan until softened. Return beef to pan; stir until heated through.
5 Meanwhile, warm tortillas according to manufacturer's instructions.
6 Divide beef mixture among serving plates; serve with tortillas, guacamole and salsa.
guacamole Roughly mash avocado; combine in small with juice, finely chopped onion and finely chopped coriander.
salsa cruda Seed then finely chop tomatoes; combine in small bowl with finely chopped chilli, finely chopped onion, juice and coriander.

preparation time 20 minutes
cooking time 15 minutes
serves 4
nutritional count per serving 31.5g total fat (7.6g saturated fat); 3089kJ (739 cal); 62.7g carbohydrate; 46.2g protein; 8.9g fibre

meat

chilli and honey barbecued steak with coleslaw

2 tablespoons barbecue sauce
1 tablespoon worcestershire sauce
1 tablespoon honey
1 fresh long red chilli, chopped finely
1 clove garlic, crushed
4 x 200g beef new-york cut steaks
coleslaw
2 tablespoons mayonnaise
1 tablespoon white wine vinegar
2 cups (160g) finely shredded white cabbage
1 cup (160g) finely shredded red cabbage
1 medium carrot (120g), grated coarsely
3 thinly sliced green onions

1 Combine sauces, honey, chilli and garlic in large bowl; add beef, turn to coat in honey mixture.
2 Make coleslaw.
3 Cook beef on heated oiled grill plate (or grill or barbecue) until browned both sides and cooked as desired.
4 Serve steaks with coleslaw.
coleslaw Place mayonnaise and vinegar in screw-top jar; shake well. Place dressing in large bowl with cabbages, carrot and onions; toss to combine.

preparation time 15 minutes
cooking time 10 minutes
serves 4
nutritional count per serving 15.2g total fat (5.4g saturated fat); 1605kJ (383 cal); 16.6g carbohydrate; 44g protein; 3.6g fibre

meat

herbed rib-eye with tapenade mash

4 large potatoes (1.2kg), chopped coarsely
1 tablespoon dried italian herbs
1 clove garlic, crushed
2 tablespoons olive oil
4 x 200g beef rib-eye steaks
½ cup (125ml) cream
2 tablespoons black olive tapenade
60g baby rocket leaves

1 Boil, steam or microwave potato until tender; drain. Cover to keep warm.
2 Meanwhile, combine herbs, garlic, oil and beef in medium bowl.
3 Cook beef on heated oiled grill plate (or grill or barbecue), brushing occasionally with herb mixture, until cooked as desired. Remove from heat, cover; stand 5 minutes.
4 Mash potato in large bowl with cream and tapenade. Stir in half the rocket.
5 Serve beef with mash and remaining rocket.

preparation time 10 minutes
cooking time 25 minutes
serves 4
nutritional count per serving 34g total fat (14.3g saturated fat); 2930kJ (761 cal); 41.1g carbohydrate; 54.6g protein; 6.4g fibre

meat

saltimbocca

8 x 100g beef scotch fillet steaks
4 slices prosciutto (60g), halved crossways
8 fresh sage leaves
½ cup (40g) finely grated pecorino cheese
40g butter
1 cup (250ml) dry white wine
1 tablespoon coarsely chopped fresh sage

1 Place beef on board; using meat mallet, flatten slightly. Centre one piece prosciutto, one sage leaf and an eighth of the cheese on each piece of beef; fold in half, secure with a toothpick.
2 Melt half the butter in large frying pan; cook saltimbocca about 5 minutes or until cooked through. Remove from pan; cover to keep warm.
3 Pour wine into same pan; bring to the boil. Boil, uncovered, until liquid is reduced by half. Stir in remaining butter and chopped sage.
4 Serve saltimbocca, drizzled with sauce, with steamed baby green beans, if you like.

preparation time 10 minutes
cooking time 25 minutes
serves 4
nutritional count per serving 21.4g total fat (11.6g saturated fat); 1777kJ (425 cal); 0.3g carbohydrate; 47.5g protein; 0g fibre

meat

veal scaloppine with salsa verde

2 tablespoons olive oil
8 veal escalopes (800g) (see note, below)
salsa verde
1 cup coarsely chopped fresh flat-leaf parley
½ cup finely chopped fresh dill
½ cup finely chopped fresh chives
2 tablespoons wholegrain mustard
⅓ cup (80ml) olive oil
¼ cup (60ml) lemon juice
¼ cup (50g) rinsed drained baby capers
2 cloves garlic, crushed

1 Make salsa verde.
2 Heat oil in large frying pan; cook veal, in batches, until browned both sides and cooked as desired.
3 Serve veal topped with salsa verde. Goes well with steamed baby new potatoes, if you like.
salsa verde Combine ingredients in medium bowl.

preparation time 15 minutes
cooking time 5 minutes
serves 4
nutritional count per serving 32.4g total fat (5.3g saturated fat); 2002kJ (479 cal); 2.2g carbohydrate; 44g protein; 1.6g fibre
note Veal escalopes are thinly sliced steaks available plain (uncrumbed) or crumbed (also known as schnitzel); we use plain (uncrumbed) in our recipes unless stated otherwise.

tip Mashed potato goes great with this recipe. Boil, steam or microwave 1kg chopped potato until tender; drain. Mash in large bowl until smooth with ⅔ cup warmed cream.

meat

rosemary lamb skewers

8 sprigs fresh rosemary
600g lamb mince
1 egg yolk
2 cloves garlic, crushed
1 tablespoon tomato paste
⅓ cup (25g) stale breadcrumbs
¼ cup (60ml) olive oil
1 large brown onion (200g), sliced thinly
1 tablespoon plain flour
1 cup (250ml) beef stock
2 medium tomatoes (300g), chopped coarsely

1 Remove two-thirds of the leaves from the bottom part of each rosemary sprig to make skewers. Finely chop 2 teaspoons of the leaves and reserve.
2 Combine mince, egg yolk, garlic, paste, breadcrumbs and reserved rosemary in medium bowl. Shape lamb mixture into sausage shapes on rosemary skewers.
3 Heat 1 tablespoon of the oil in large frying pan; cook skewers until browned and cooked through. Cover to keep warm.
4 Heat remaining oil in same pan; cook onion, stirring, until soft. Add flour; cook, stirring, until mixture bubbles and thickens. Gradually stir in stock until smooth. Add tomato; cook, stirring, until gravy boils and thickens.
5 Serve rosemary lamb skewers with gravy.

preparation time 15 minutes
cooking time 20 minutes
serves 4
nutritional count per serving 26g total fat (7.1g saturated fat); 1781kJ (426 cal); 11.9g carbohydrate; 35.1g protein; 2.5g fibre

meat

souvlaki with tomato, almond and mint salad

¼ cup (60ml) olive oil
2 teaspoons finely grated lemon rind
¼ cup (60ml) lemon juice
¼ cup finely chopped fresh oregano
800g lamb fillets, cut into 3cm pieces
2 medium yellow capsicums (400g), chopped coarsely
1 medium red onion (150g), chopped coarsely
2 large tomatoes (440g), chopped coarsely
¼ cup (35g) slivered almonds, toasted
1 cup firmly packed fresh mint leaves

1 Combine oil, rind, juice and oregano in screw-top jar; shake well.
2 Thread lamb, capsicum and onion, alternately, on skewers. Place on baking tray; drizzle with half the dressing. Cook souvlaki on heated oiled grill plate (or grill or barbecue) until cooked as desired.
3 Meanwhile, combine tomato, nuts and mint with the remaining dressing in small bowl.
4 Serve souvlaki with tomato, almond and mint salad, and warmed pitta bread, if you like.

preparation time 20 minutes
cooking time 15 minutes
serves 4
nutritional count per serving 26.1g total fat (5.5g saturated fat); 1914kJ (458 cal); 7.8g carbohydrate; 46.2g protein; 4.3g fibre
tip To toast nuts, place in a single layer in a dry pan and stir over a low heat about 3-5 minutes or until fragrant and just changed in colour. Be careful to avoid burning nuts.

meat

lamb racks with mustard maple glaze

4 x 4 french-trimmed lamb cutlet racks (720g)
2 cloves garlic, sliced thinly
2 medium parsnips (500g), cut into 2cm cubes
2 small kumara (500g), cut into 2cm cubes
½ cup loosely packed fresh flat-leaf parsley leaves
mustard maple glaze
50g butter
⅓ cup (80ml) maple syrup
2 tablespoons wholegrain mustard

1 Preheat oven to 200°C/180°C fan-forced.
2 Make mustard maple glaze.
3 Meanwhile, using sharp knife, make cuts in lamb; press garlic slices into cuts. Place lamb in large oiled baking dish; brush with 2 tablespoons of the glaze.
4 Combine remaining glaze, parsnip and kumara in medium bowl.
5 Place vegetables in baking dish with lamb; roast, uncovered, about 15 minutes or until vegetables are tender and lamb is cooked as desired. Stir parsley into vegetables; serve with lamb.
mustard maple glaze Combine ingredients in small saucepan; cook, stirring, until slightly thickened.

preparation time 10 minutes
cooking time 20 minutes
serves 4
nutritional count per serving 26.2g total fat (13.8g saturated fat); 2153kJ (515 cal); 44.4g carbohydrate; 22.8g protein; 5.5g fibre

meat

lamb teriyaki with broccolini

1 tablespoon vegetable oil
800g lamb strips
4 green onions, chopped coarsely
3cm piece fresh ginger (15g), grated
175g broccolini, chopped coarsely
150g green beans, trimmed, halved crossways
⅓ cup (80ml) teriyaki sauce
2 tablespoons honey
2 teaspoons sesame oil
1 tablespoon toasted sesame seeds

1 Heat half the vegetable oil in wok; stir-fry lamb, in batches, until browned.
2 Heat remaining vegetable oil in wok; stir-fry onion and ginger until onion softens. Add broccolini and beans; stir-fry until vegetables are tender. Remove from wok.
3 Add sauce, honey and sesame oil to wok; bring to the boil. Boil, uncovered, about 3 minutes or until sauce thickens slightly. Return lamb and vegetables to wok; stir-fry until hot. Sprinkle with seeds. Serve with steamed rice, if you like.

preparation time 10 minutes
cooking time 15 minutes
serves 4
nutritional count per serving 15.9g total fat (4.3g saturated fat); 1626kJ (389 cal); 14.1g carbohydrate; 45.7g protein; 3.4g fibre
tip To toast sesame seeds, place in a dry pan and stir over a low heat about 3-5 minutes or until fragrant and just changed in colour.

tip Tzatziki is a Greek yogurt dip made with cucumber, garlic and sometimes chopped fresh mint. You can buy tzatziki ready-made in supermarkets and delis.

meat

spiced lamb burger with tzatziki

500g lamb mince
½ small red onion (50g), chopped finely
1 egg yolk
½ cup (35g) stale breadcrumbs
2 tablespoons sumac
1 large loaf turkish bread (430g)
250g tzatziki
350g watercress, trimmed
¼ cup (60ml) lemon juice
225g can sliced beetroot, drained

1 Combine lamb, onion, egg yolk, breadcrumbs and half the sumac in medium bowl; shape mixture into four patties.
2 Cook patties on heated oiled grill plate (or grill or barbecue) until cooked.
3 Meanwhile, preheat grill. Trim ends from bread; cut remaining bread into quarters then halve pieces horizontally. Toast, cut-sides up, under grill.
4 Combine remaining sumac and tzatziki in small bowl. Combine watercress and juice in another bowl.
5 Sandwich patties, tzatziki mixture, beetroot and watercress between bread pieces.

preparation time 20 minutes
cooking time 10 minutes
serves 4
nutritional count per serving 21.1g total fat (7.5g saturated fat); 2604kJ (623 cal); 60g carbohydrate; 43.8g protein; 8g fibre
note Sumac is a purple-red, astringent spice ground from berries growing on shrubs that flourish wild around the Mediterranean. It adds a tart, lemony flavour to dishes. It's found in major supermarkets, spice shops and Middle-Eastern food stores.

meat

lamb, bocconcini and gremolata stacks

4 x 150g lamb leg steaks
1 tablespoon olive oil
1 large red capsicum (350g)
2 tablespoons lemon juice
100g bocconcini cheese, sliced thinly
gremolata
2 teaspoons finely grated lemon rind
2 cloves garlic, chopped finely
2 tablespoons finely chopped fresh basil

1 Make gremolata.
2 Using meat mallet, gently pound lamb between sheets of plastic wrap until 1cm thick. Heat oil in large frying pan; cook lamb, in batches, until cooked as desired. Place lamb on oven tray.
3 Meanwhile, quarter capsicum, discard seeds and membranes. Roast under grill, skin-side up, until skin blisters and blackens. Cover capsicum pieces in plastic or paper for 5 minutes; peel away skin. Combine capsicum and juice in small bowl.
4 Meanwhile, preheat grill.
5 Top steaks with capsicum then cheese; grill about 5 minutes or until cheese melts. Serve stacks sprinkled with gremolata and, if you like, a salad of baby rocket leaves.
gremolata Combine ingredients in small bowl.

preparation time 15 minutes
cooking time 20 minutes
serves 4
nutritional count per serving 16.7g total fat (6.8g saturated fat); 1346kJ (322 cal); 3.4g carbohydrate; 38.8g protein; 1.2g fibre

tip Roasted capsicum pieces are also available from delis, or in jars, covered in oil or brine, from many supermarkets.

meat

stir-fried pork with buk choy and rice noodles

¼ cup (60ml) oyster sauce
2 tablespoons light soy sauce
2 tablespoons sweet sherry
1 tablespoon brown sugar
1 clove garlic, crushed
1 star anise, crushed
pinch five-spice powder
400g fresh rice noodles
2 teaspoons sesame oil
600g pork fillets, sliced thinly
700g baby buk choy, chopped coarsely

1 Combine sauces, sherry, sugar, garlic, star anise and five-spice in small jug.
2 Place noodles in large heatproof bowl, cover with boiling water; separate with fork, drain.
3 Heat oil in wok; stir-fry pork, in batches, until cooked as desired. Return pork to wok with sauce mixture, noodles and buk choy; stir-fry until buk choy is wilted.

preparation time 10 minutes
cooking time 10 minutes
serves 4
nutritional count per serving 6.7g total fat (1.6g saturated fat); 1492kJ (357 cal); 31.6g carbohydrate; 37.9g protein; 2.9g fibre

pasta

warm pasta provençale salad

375g rigatoni pasta
600g lamb fillets
¾ cup (115g) seeded black olives, halved
1 cup (150g) drained semi-dried tomatoes in oil, chopped coarsely
400g can artichoke hearts, drained, halved
1 small red onion (100g), sliced thinly
60g baby rocket leaves
½ cup (120g) green olive tapenade
2 tablespoons olive oil
2 tablespoons lemon juice

1 Cook pasta in large saucepan of boiling water until tender.
2 Meanwhile, cook lamb, uncovered, in heated oiled large frying pan until cooked as desired. Cover; stand 5 minutes then slice thickly.
3 Combine drained pasta with lamb and remaining ingredients in large bowl. Serve warm.

preparation time 15 minutes
cooking time 15 minutes
serves 6
nutritional count per serving 16.9g total fat (3.4g saturated fat); 2203kJ (527 cal); 57.4g carbohydrate; 32g protein; 7.5g fibre

tip Rigatoni is a tube-shaped pasta with ridges on the outside; penne can be substituted. Tapenade is a thick olive paste. Use black olive tapenade if you prefer.

pasta

ravioli with tomato, pea and basil sauce

2 teaspoons olive oil
6 slices pancetta (90g)
1 clove garlic, crushed
700g bottled tomato pasta sauce
¼ cup (60ml) dry white wine
2 tablespoons finely chopped fresh basil
1 cup (120g) frozen peas
625g spinach and ricotta ravioli

1 Heat oil in large frying pan; cook pancetta until crisp. Drain on absorbent paper; break into pieces.
2 Cook garlic in same pan, stirring, 1 minute. Add sauce, wine and basil; bring to the boil. Add peas, reduce heat; simmer, uncovered, 15 minutes.
3 Meanwhile, cook ravioli in large saucepan of boiling water, uncovered, until just tender; drain. Return ravioli to pan, add sauce; toss to combine. Divide among serving bowls; top with pancetta.

preparation time 10 minutes
cooking time 15 minutes
serves 4
nutritional count per serving 12.8g total fat (4.1g saturated fat); 1593kJ (381 cal); 46.6g carbohydrate; 20.1g protein; 7.4g fibre
note Pancetta is an Italian unsmoked bacon available from delicatessens; pork belly cured in salt and spices then rolled into a sausage shape and dried for several weeks. It is used, sliced or chopped, as an ingredient rather than eaten on its own. Bacon can be substituted for the pancetta, if you prefer.

pasta

lemon, pea and ricotta pasta

375g angel hair pasta
2 cups (240g) frozen peas
2 tablespoons olive oil
2 cloves garlic, sliced thinly
2 teaspoons finely grated lemon rind
½ cup (125ml) lemon juice
¾ cup (180g) ricotta cheese, crumbled

1 Cook pasta in large saucepan of boiling water until tender; add peas during last minute of pasta cooking time. Drain, reserving ¼ cup cooking liquid. Rinse pasta and peas under cold water; drain.
2 Meanwhile, heat oil in small frying pan; cook garlic, stirring, until fragrant.
3 Combine pasta and peas in large bowl with reserved cooking liquid, garlic, rind and juice; stir in cheese.

preparation time 5 minutes
cooking time 10 minutes
serves 4
nutritional count per serving 15.6g total fat (4.7g saturated fat); 2123kJ (508 cal); 69g carbohydrate; 19g protein; 6.9g fibre

tip Fetta cheese can be used in place of the ricotta cheese. Stir ⅓ cup loosely packed fresh mint leaves into this recipe to add a fresh minty flavour, if you like.

tip This recipe freezes well; you could double the recipe and freeze one batch for a rainy day.

pasta

macaroni cheese with olives

375g elbow macaroni
60g butter
1 small red onion (100g), sliced thinly
1 clove garlic, crushed
1 medium red capsicum (200g), sliced thinly
150g button mushrooms, sliced thinly
⅓ cup (50g) plain flour
3 cups (750ml) milk
⅓ cup (95g) tomato paste
⅓ cup (40g) seeded black olives, halved
½ cup finely chopped fresh basil
1½ cups (150g) coarsely grated pizza cheese

1 Cook pasta in large saucepan of boiling water until just tender; drain.
2 Meanwhile, melt butter in large saucepan; cook onion, garlic, capsicum and mushrooms, stirring, until vegetables soften. Add flour; cook, stirring, until mixture bubbles and thickens. Gradually stir in milk. Add paste; cook, stirring, until sauce boils and thickens.
3 Preheat grill.
4 Stir pasta, olives, basil and half the cheese into sauce. Place mixture in deep 2-litre (8-cup) ovenproof dish; sprinkle with remaining cheese. Grill until cheese melts and is browned lightly.
5 Serve macaroni with a baby spinach, grape tomato and celery salad, if you like, for a delicious family dinner.

preparation time 10 minutes
cooking time 25 minutes
serves 4
nutritional count per serving 29.5g total fat (18.4g saturated fat); 3223kJ (771 cal); 90.1g carbohydrate; 32.4g protein; 6.7g fibre

rice

chilli fried rice with chicken and broccolini

You need to cook 1 cup (200g) white long-grain rice the day before making this recipe. Spread it in a thin layer on a tray and refrigerate it overnight. You also need a large barbecued chicken, weighing approximately 900g.

1 tablespoon peanut oil
3 eggs, beaten lightly
1 medium brown onion (150g), sliced thinly
1 clove garlic, crushed
2 fresh long red chillies, sliced thinly
175g broccolini, chopped coarsely
2 cups (320g) shredded barbecued chicken
3 cups cooked white long-grain rice
1 tablespoon light soy sauce
1 tablespoon hoisin sauce

1 Heat about a third of the oil in wok; add half the egg, swirl wok to make a thin omelette. Remove omelette from wok; roll then cut into thin strips. Repeat process using another third of the oil and remaining egg.
2 Heat remaining oil in wok; stir-fry onion, garlic and chilli until onion softens. Add broccolini; stir-fry until tender.
3 Add remaining ingredients to wok; stir-fry until hot. Add omelette; toss gently.

preparation time 10 minutes
cooking time 15 minutes
serves 4
nutritional count per serving 15.3g total fat (3.8g saturated fat); 1881kJ (450 cal); 44.6g carbohydrate; 30.9g protein; 4.1g fibre

tips If you don't have any leftover cooked rice, cook 2 cups (400g) white long-grain rice the day before making this recipe. Spread it in a thin layer on a tray and refrigerate it overnight. *Dried chinese sausages,* also called lop chong, are usually made from pork and are sold, strung together, in Asian food stores.

rice

nasi goreng

Nasi goreng, which translates simply as "fried rice" in Indonesia and Malaysia, was first created to use up yesterday's leftovers.

720g cooked medium king prawns
1 tablespoon peanut oil
175g dried chinese sausages, sliced thickly
1 medium brown onion (150g), sliced thinly
1 medium red capsicum (200g), sliced thinly
2 fresh long red chillies, sliced thinly
2 cloves garlic, crushed
2cm piece fresh ginger (10g), grated
1 teaspoon shrimp paste
4 cups (600g) cold cooked white long-grain rice
2 tablespoons kecap manis
1 tablespoon light soy sauce
4 green onions, sliced thinly
1 tablespoon peanut oil, extra
4 eggs

1 Shell and devein prawns.
2 Heat half the oil in wok; stir-fry sausage, in batches, until browned.
3 Heat remaining oil in wok; stir-fry onion, capsicum, chilli, garlic, ginger and paste, until vegetables soften. Add prawns and rice; stir-fry 2 minutes. Return sausage to wok with sauces and half the green onion; stir-fry until combined and heated through.
4 Heat extra oil in large frying pan; fry eggs, one side only, until just set. Divide nasi goreng among serving plates, top each with an egg; sprinkle with remaining green onion.

preparation time 20 minutes
cooking time 15 minutes
serves 4
nutritional count per serving 25.7g total fat (7.4g saturated fat); 2730kJ (653 cal); 48.5g carbohydrate; 54.7g protein; 3.3g fibre

rice

chicken, lentil and cauliflower pilaf

1 medium brown onion (150g), sliced thinly
1 clove garlic, crushed
2 tablespoons madras curry paste (see note, below)
1 cup (200g) basmati rice
½ small cauliflower (500g), cut into florets
400g can brown lentils, rinsed, drained
1 cup (250ml) chicken stock
1 cup (250ml) water
2 cups (320g) coarsely chopped barbecued chicken
½ cup firmly packed fresh coriander leaves

1 Cook onion and garlic in heated oiled large frying pan until onion softens. Add paste; cook, stirring, about 5 minutes or until fragrant.
2 Add rice, cauliflower and lentils to pan; stir to coat in onion mixture. Add stock, the water and chicken; bring to the boil. Reduce heat; simmer, covered tightly, about 15 minutes or until rice is tender and liquid has been absorbed.
3 Remove from heat; fluff pilaf with fork. Stir in coriander; serve with lime wedges, pappadums and lime pickle, if you like.

preparation time 10 minutes
cooking time 20 minutes
serves 4
nutritional count per serving 10.7g total fat (2.3g saturated fat); 1814kJ (434 cal); 50.2g carbohydrate; 36.6g protein; 6.1g fibre
notes Commercially prepared curry pastes can vary in heat and flavour. Add less than recommended to suit your spice level tolerance if not used to hot curry flavours.
Lime pickle is an Indian special mixed pickle/condiment of limes that adds a hot and spicy taste to meals especially rice.

tip Buy a barbecued chicken weighing approximately 900g on your way home from work; skin and bone it then chop the meat to get the right amount of chicken required for this recipe.

glossary

angel hair pasta also known as barbina. Long, thin, strands of spaghetti-like pasta. They are called "capelli d'angelo" in Italian.

bean, four-bean mix made with kidney beans, butter beans, chickpeas and cannellini beans.

beef
  eye-fillet tenderloin fillet with a fine texture; a tender, though expensive, cut.
  scotch fillet cut from the muscle running behind the shoulder along the spine.
  new-york cut boneless striploin steak.
  rib-eye steaks also known as beef scotch fillet steak.

beetroot also known as red beets or just beets; firm, round root vegetable.

breadcrumbs stale one- or two-day-old bread made into crumbs by grating, blending or processing.

broccolini a cross between broccoli and chinese kale; milder and sweeter than broccoli. If not available substitute with broccoli.

buk choy, baby also known as pak kat farang or shanghai bok choy, is smaller and more tender than buk choy. Its mildly acrid, distinctively appealing taste has made it one of the most commonly used asian greens.

butter use salted or unsalted (sweet) butter; 125g is equal to one stick (4 ounces).

buttermilk originally just the liquid left after cream was separated from milk, today it is commercially made similarly to yogurt.

capsicum also known as bell pepper or, simply, pepper. Discard membranes and seeds before use.

cheese
  pecorino is the generic italian name for cheeses made from sheep milk. It's a hard, white to pale-yellow cheese. If you can't find it, use parmesan.
  pizza a commercial blend of processed grated mozzarella, cheddar and parmesan cheeses.

chicken schnitzel breast fillets are cut horizontally in half then pounded between layers of plastic until they are thin and of an even thickness.

coriander also known as pak chee, cilantro or chinese parsley; bright-green leafy herb with a pungent flavour.

cream we used fresh cream, also known as pure cream and pouring cream, unless otherwise stated.

cucumber, lebanese short, slender and thin-skinned. Probably the most popular variety because of its tender, edible skin, tiny, yielding seeds, and sweet, fresh and flavoursome taste.

cumin also known as zeera or comino; has a spicy, nutty flavour.

five-spice powder a fragrant mixture of ground cinnamon, cloves, star anise, sichuan pepper and fennel seeds. Also known as chinese five-spice.

flour, plain an all-purpose flour made from wheat.

kaffir lime leaves also known as bai magrood, sold fresh, dried or frozen; looks like two glossy dark-green leaves joined end to end, forming a rounded hourglass shape. A strip of fresh lime peel may be substituted for each kaffir lime leaf.

kipfler potatoes small, finger-shaped potato having a nutty flavour.

kumara Polynesian name of orange-fleshed sweet potato often confused with yam.

lamb fillets the larger fillet from a row of loin chops or cutlets. Also known as backstrap.

maple syrup a thin syrup distilled from the sap of the maple tree. Maple-flavoured syrup or pancake syrup is not an adequate substitute for the real thing.

mince ground meat.

mustard, wholegrain also known as seeded.

noodles
  fresh rice also known as ho fun, khao pun, sen yau, pho or kway tiau. Can be purchased in strands of various widths or large sheets weighing about 500g.

hokkien also known as stir-fry noodles; fresh wheat noodles resembling thick, yellow-brown spaghetti.

onions
  green also known as scallion or, incorrectly, shallot; an immature onion picked before the bulb has formed, having a long, bright-green edible stalk.
  red also known as spanish, red spanish or bermuda onion; a sweet-flavoured, large, purple-red onion.

parsley, flat-leaf also known as continental parsley or italian parsley.

prawns also known as shrimp.

rocket also known as arugula, rugula and rucola; a green peppery-tasting leaf. Baby rocket leaves, also known as wild rocket, are both smaller and less peppery.

sambal oelek (also ulek or olek) Indonesian in origin; a salty paste made from ground chillies and vinegar.

sauces
  barbecue a spicy, tomato-based sauce.
  fish also called nam pla or nuoc nam; made from pulverised salted fermented fish, most often anchovies. Has a pungent smell and strong taste; use sparingly.
  hoisin a thick, sweet and spicy Chinese sauce made from salted fermented soya beans, onions and garlic.
  soy made from fermented soya beans. Several variations are available in most supermarkets and Asian food stores.
  kecap manis a dark, thick sweet soy sauce used in most South-East Asian cuisines. Depending on the brand, the soy's sweetness is derived from the addition of either molasses or palm sugar when brewed.
  light soy is fairly thin in consistency and, while paler than the others, the saltiest tasting; used in dishes in which the natural colour of the ingredients is to be maintained. Not to be confused with salt-reduced or low-sodium soy sauces.
  oyster Asian in origin, this rich, brown sauce is made from oysters and their brine, cooked with salt and soy sauce, and thickened with starches.
  plum a thick, sweet and sour dipping sauce made from plums, vinegar, sugar, chillies and spices.
  sweet chilli a comparatively mild, Thai-style sauce made from red chillies, sugar, garlic and vinegar.
  teriyaki one of Japan's favourite sauces; made from soy sauce, mirin, sugar, ginger and other spices, and imparts a distinctive glaze when brushed over grilled meat or poultry.
  tomato pasta sauce prepared sauce made from a blend of tomatoes, herbs and spices.
  worcestershire a dark coloured condiment made from garlic, soy sauce, tamarind, onions, molasses, lime, anchovies, vinegar and seasonings. Available in most supermarkets.

shrimp paste also known as kapi, trasi and blanchan; a strong-scented, very firm preserved paste made of salted dried shrimp.

spinach also known as english spinach and, incorrectly, silver beet.

star anise dried star-shaped pod having an astringent aniseed flavour; used to favour stocks and marinades. Available whole and ground, it is an essential ingredient in five-spice powder.

sugar
  palm sugar also known as nam tan pip, jaggery, jawa or gula melaka; made from the sap of the sugar palm tree. Substitute it with brown sugar if unavailable.
  white a coarse, granulated table sugar, also known as crystal sugar.

turkish bread also known as pide; comes in long (about 45cm) flat loaves as well as individual rounds.

zucchini also known as courgette; belongs to the squash family.

conversion chart

MEASURES

One Australian metric measuring cup holds approximately 250ml, one Australian metric tablespoon holds 20ml, one Australian metric teaspoon holds 5ml.

The difference between one country's measuring cups and another's is within a 2- or 3-teaspoon variance, and will not affect your cooking results. North America, New Zealand and the United Kingdom use a 15ml tablespoon. All cup and spoon measurements are level. The most accurate way of measuring dry ingredients is to weigh them. When measuring liquids, use a clear glass or plastic jug with metric markings.

We use large eggs with an average weight of 60g.

DRY MEASURES

METRIC	IMPERIAL
15g	½oz
30g	1oz
60g	2oz
90g	3oz
125g	4oz (¼lb)
155g	5oz
185g	6oz
220g	7oz
250g	8oz (½lb)
280g	9oz
315g	10oz
345g	11oz
375g	12oz (¾lb)
410g	13oz
440g	14oz
470g	15oz
500g	16oz (1lb)
750g	24oz (1½lb)
1kg	32oz (2lb)

LIQUID MEASURES

METRIC	IMPERIAL
30ml	1 fluid oz
60ml	2 fluid oz
100ml	3 fluid oz
125ml	4 fluid oz
150ml	5 fluid oz (¼ pint/1 gill)
190ml	6 fluid oz
250ml	8 fluid oz
300ml	10 fluid oz (½ pint)
500ml	16 fluid oz
600ml	20 fluid oz (1 pint)
1000ml (1 litre)	1¾ pints

LENGTH MEASURES

METRIC	IMPERIAL
3mm	⅛in
6mm	¼in
1cm	½in
2cm	¾in
2.5cm	1in
5cm	2in
6cm	2½in
8cm	3in
10cm	4in
13cm	5in
15cm	6in
18cm	7in
20cm	8in
23cm	9in
25cm	10in
28cm	11in
30cm	12in (1ft)

OVEN TEMPERATURES

These oven temperatures are only a guide for conventional ovens. For fan-forced ovens, check the manufacturer's manual.

	°C (CELSIUS)	°F (FAHRENHEIT)	GAS MARK
Very slow	120	250	½
Slow	150	275-300	1-2
Moderately slow	160	325	3
Moderate	180	350-375	4-5
Moderately hot	200	400	6
Hot	220	425-450	7-8
Very hot	240	475	9

index

B
beef
  chilli and honey barbecued steak 25
  fajitas with guacamole and salsa cruda 22
  herbed rib-eye with tapenade mash 26
  saltimbocca 29
  spicy beef and bean salad 21
burger, spiced lamb, with tzatziki 41

C
chicken
  chicken margherita 14
  chicken, lentil and cauliflower pilaf 59
  chilli fried rice with chicken and broccolini 54
  ginger-plum chicken and noodle stir-fry 13
  herbed chicken schnitzel 18
  pesto chicken with grilled zucchini 10
  spinach and ricotta-stuffed chicken parmigiana 17
chips, homemade 16
coleslaw 25
couscous, lemon pistachio 5

F
fajitas with guacamole and salsa cruda 22
fish
  fish cutlets with mango salsa 6
  fish with chunky tomato, anchovy and caper sauce 2
  grilled snapper fillets with fennel and onion salad 9
  spiced fried fish 5
fried rice, chilli, with chicken and broccolini 54

G
ginger-plum chicken and noodle stir-fry 13

glaze, mustard maple 37
gremolata 42
guacamole 22

L
lamb
  lamb, bocconcini and gremolata stacks 42
  lamb racks with mustard maple glaze 37
  lamb teriyaki with broccolini 38
  rosemary lamb skewers 33
  souvlaki with tomato, almond and mint salad 34
  spiced lamb burger with tzatziki 41
  warm pasta provençale salad 46
lemon pistachio couscous 5
lemon, pea and ricotta pasta 50

M
macaroni cheese with olives 53
mango salsa 6
margherita chicken 14
mash, tapenade, with herbed rib-eye 26
mash, potato 32
mustard maple glaze 37

N
nasi goreng 57

P
parmigiana, spinach and ricotta-stuffed chicken 17
pasta
  lemon, pea and ricotta pasta 50
  macaroni cheese with olives 53
  ravioli with tomato, pea and basil sauce 49
  warm pasta provençale salad 46
pesto chicken with grilled zucchini 10

pilaf, chicken, lentil and cauliflower 59
pork with buk choy and rice noodles, stir-fried 45
potato, mashed 32

R
ravioli with tomato, pea and basil sauce 49
rice
  chicken, lentil and cauliflower pilaf 59
  chilli fried rice with chicken and broccolini 54
  nasi goreng 57

S
salad
  fennel and onion, with grilled snapper fillets 9
  green bean 18
  souvlaki with tomato, almond and mint 34
  spicy beef and bean 21
  warm pasta provençale 46
salsa cruda 22
salsa verde 30
salsa, mango 6
saltimbocca 29
scaloppine, veal, with salsa verde 30
schnitzel, herbed chicken 18
skewers, rosemary lamb 33
skewers, souvlaki with tomato, almond and mint salad 34
souvlaki with tomato, almond and mint salad 34
stir-fried pork with buk choy and rice noodles 45
stir-fry, ginger-plum chicken and noodle 13

T
teriyaki lamb with broccolini 38

V
veal scaloppine with salsa verde 30

ACP BOOKS
General manager Christine Whiston
Editorial director Susan Tomnay
Creative director Hieu Chi Nguyen
Art director Hannah Blackmore
Designer Caryl Wiggins
Senior editor Wendy Bryant
Food director Pamela Clark
Test Kitchen manager Belinda Farlow
Director of sales Brian Cearnes
Marketing manager Bridget Cody
Communications and brand manager Xanthe Roberts
Senior business analyst Rebecca Varela
Circulation manager Jama Mclean
Operations manager David Scotto
Production manager Victoria Jefferys
European rights enquiries Laura Bamford
lbamford@acpuk.com

acp books

ACP Books are published by ACP Magazines
a division of PBL Media Pty Limited
Group editorial director, Women's lifestyle Pat Ingram
Group publishing & sales director, Women's lifestyle Lynette Phillips
Commercial manager, Women's lifestyle Seymour Cohen
Marketing director, Women's lifestyle Matthew Dominello
Research director, Women's lifestyle Justin Stone
PBL Media, Chief Executive Officer Ian Law

Cover Lamb racks with mustard maple glaze, page 37
Photographer Rob Palmer
Stylist Michaela le Compte
Food preparation Angela Muscat

Produced by ACP Books, Sydney.
Published by ACP Books,
a division of ACP Magazines Ltd,
54 Park St, Sydney; GPO Box 4088,
Sydney, NSW 2001
phone (02) 9282 8618; fax (02) 9267 9438.
acpbooks@acpmagazines.com.au
www.acpbooks.com.au
Printed by Dai Nippon in Korea.
Australia Distributed by Network Services, phone +61 2 9282 8777; fax +61 2 9264 3278
networkweb@networkservicescompany.com.au
United Kingdom Distributed by Australian Consolidated Press (UK),
phone (01604) 642 200; fax (01604) 642 300; books@acpuk.com
New Zealand Distributed by Netlink Distribution Company, phone (9) 366 9966; ask@ndc.co.nz
South Africa Distributed by PSD Promotions,
phone (27 11) 392 6065/6/7; fax (27 11) 392 6079/80; orders@psdprom.co.za
Canada Distributed by Publishers Group Canada,
phone (800) 663 5714; fax (800) 565 3770; service@raincoast.com

Title: Fast dinners / food director, Pamela Clark.
ISBN: 978 1 86396 851 5 (pbk.)
Series: The working mum.
Notes: Includes index.
Subjects: Quick and easy cookery.
Other Authors/Contributors: Clark, Pamela.
Also Titled: Australian women's weekly.
Dewey Number: 641.555
© ACP Magazines Ltd 2009
ABN 18 053 273 546
This publication is copyright. No part of it may be reproduced or transmitted
in any form without the written permission of the publishers.
Send recipe enquiries to:
recipeenquiries@acpmagazines.com.au